Reindeer

by Dee Phillips

Consultants:

Perry S. Barboza, Professor of Biology
Institute of Arctic Biology, University of Alaska Fairbanks

Kimberly Brenneman, PhD
National Institute for Early Education Research, Rutgers University, New Brunswick, New Jersey

BEARPORT
PUBLISHING

New York, New York

Credits

Cover, © Andreas Gradin/Shutterstock; 2–3, © Sergey Krasnoshchokov/Shutterstock; 4, © Karl Umbriaco/Shutterstock; 5, © Yva Momatiuk & John Eastcott/Minden Pictures/FLPA; 6, © Sergey Krasnoshchokov/Shutterstock; 7, © Michael Quinton/Minden Pictures/FLPA; 8, © Sergey Krasnoshchokov/Shutterstock; 9, © Alaska.com/Alamy; 10T, © TTPhoto/Shutterstock; 10B, © Bildagentur Zoonar GmbH/Shutterstock; 11, © Jeff McGraw/Shutterstock; 12, © Incredible Arctic/Shutterstock; 13, © Donald M. Jones/Minden Pictures/FLPA; 14, © Rumo/Shutterstock; 15, © Hillebrand Breuker/Minden Pictures/FLPA; 16–17, © Alex Uralsky/Shutterstock and © Imagebroker/Shutterstock; 18, © Dmitri Gomon/Shutterstock; 19, © BMJ/Shutterstock; 20T, © Patricio Robles Gil/Minden Pictures/FLPA; 20B, © J.L. Klein and M.L. Hubert/FLPA; 21, © Incredible Arctic/Shutterstock; 22, © Ruby Tuesday Books; 23TC, © BMJ/Shutterstock; 23TR, © joleoi/Shutterstock; 23BL, © Incredible Arctic/Shutterstock; 23BC, © Sergey Krasnoshchokov/Shutterstock; 23BR, © Incredible Arctic/Shutterstock.

Publisher: Kenn Goin
Creative Director: Spencer Brinker
Senior Editor: Joyce Tavolacci
Photo Researcher: Ruby Tuesday Ltd.

Library of Congress Cataloging-in-Publication Data

Phillips, Dee, 1967– author.
 Reindeer / By Dee Phillips.
    pages cm. — (Arctic animals)
 Includes bibliographical references and index.
 ISBN 978-1-62724-529-6 (library binding) — ISBN 1-62724-529-4 (library binding)
 1. Reindeer—Juvenile literature. I. Title.
 QL737.U55P487 2015
 599.65'8—dc23
                                    2014035746

For more information, write to Bearport Publishing Company, Inc., 45 West 21st Street, Suite 3B, New York, New York 10010. Printed in the United States of America.

10 9 8 7 6 5 4 3 2 1

Contents

A Hidden Meal

It's an icy cold morning in the **Arctic**.

A reindeer looks for food under the deep snow.

It begins digging a hole with its large **hoof**.

The reindeer digs and digs until it reaches some food.

At last, the hungry animal can eat its breakfast.

Reindeer are also known as caribou. Both male and female reindeer have large bony antlers.

antlers

a reindeer
digging for food

A Chilly Home

Reindeer live in some of the coldest, most northern parts of the world.

Most of them live on a kind of land called the **tundra**.

This flat ground is covered with ice and snow for most of the year.

No trees grow on the tundra, and only a few tough plants can survive there.

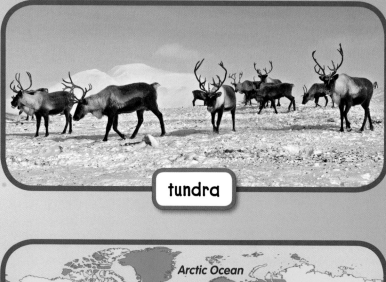

tundra

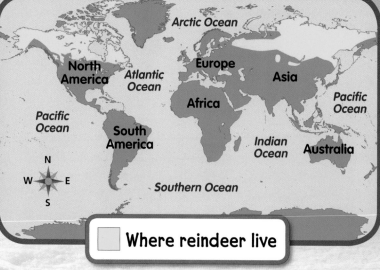

Arctic Ocean

North America

Atlantic Ocean

Europe

Asia

Africa

Pacific Ocean

Pacific Ocean

South America

Indian Ocean

Australia

Southern Ocean

N
W E
S

Where reindeer live

Some reindeer live in cold forests where evergreen trees grow. This kind of land is called the taiga.

taiga

On the Move

Reindeer live in large groups called herds.

Many herds move, or **migrate**, from place to place throughout the year.

A reindeer herd might migrate in summer to find food.

Then it might move again in winter to find a place that is less cold and windy.

a herd migrating

Some reindeer herds travel more than 3,000 miles (4,828 km) each year. If a herd comes to a river or lake, the reindeer swim across.

Finding Food

Reindeer eat different types of food during the year.

In winter, they eat a plantlike food called **lichen** that grows under the snow.

In summer, the ice and snow on the tundra melt.

For just a few weeks, plants are able to grow.

At this time of year, reindeer eat grasses and leaves.

lichen

Arctic willow leaves

In fall, lots of mushrooms grow on the tundra. Reindeer love to eat mushrooms and often run around looking for their favorite food.

Fighting in Fall

When fall arrives, the air gets cooler.

It's **mating season** for reindeer.

During this time, males, or bulls, fight each other with their large antlers.

The female reindeer mate with the bulls who are best at fighting.

The females won't have their babies, however, until spring.

A reindeer loses and grows a new pair of antlers each year. Male reindeer lose their antlers in winter. Females lose their antlers in spring.

a reindeer that has lost its antlers

male reindeer fighting

How do you think a reindeer stays warm in winter?

Warm in Winter

During fall, a reindeer grows a thick coat of hair on its body.

The hair keeps the reindeer warm during the cold and windy winter.

Even a reindeer's nose is covered with hair.

This hair protects the reindeer's nose when it eats lichen that's buried under the snow.

A reindeer's large hooves also help it survive in its chilly home. They spread out on the snow when it walks—just like snowshoes. This keeps the reindeer from sinking into soft snow.

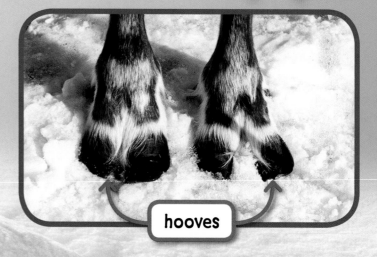

hooves

thick winter
coat

hairy
nose

15

Spring Babies

After the long, cold winter, spring finally arrives in the Arctic.

As the weather gets warmer, a reindeer's thick winter coat begins to fall out.

At the same time, a thin summer coat begins to grow.

Something else happens in spring, too.

Female reindeer give birth to their babies, or calves.

A newborn calf weighs about 13 pounds (6 kg). That's about the weight of a small dog.

Ready to Run

Almost as soon as it's born, a reindeer calf tries to stand up.

The baby's long legs are very wobbly, but it can soon walk.

Within two hours of being born, the calf can run with its mother.

Running is important—baby reindeer must be able to escape from enemies.

Wolves, bears, and wolverines all try to eat reindeer calves and adults.

a reindeer calf learning to walk

Why do you think reindeer calves are born in spring?

(The answer is on page 24.)

18

mother
reindeer

A reindeer calf drinks milk from its mother's body. The fatty milk helps the baby grow bigger and stronger every day.

a calf
drinking milk

All Grown Up

A reindeer calf grows up fast.

Just a few weeks after it is born, it starts to eat plants.

By the time it is two months old, its antlers start to grow.

The reindeer calf stays with its mother for up to two years.

Then it is ready to become a grown-up member of the herd!

antlers

a two-month-old calf

adult reindeer

An adult reindeer measures about 4 feet (1 m) from the ground to its shoulders. It can weigh as much as two or three adult humans.

a four-month-old calf

21

Science Lab

Let's investigate how a reindeer's hooves help it to walk on soft, deep snow.

Little Foot, Big Foot

You will need:
- A baking pan that's about 2 inches (5 cm) deep • Sand

1. Fill the baking pan with sand, and pat it down with your hands.

2. Now press hard on the sand with your index fingers.

   What happens to your fingers?

What do you think will happen if you press down on the sand with your whole hand?

3. Test your prediction by pressing down hard on the sand with your hands.

   What happened this time? Did your prediction match what happened?

Each of your index fingers acted like a small foot. Each of your hands was like a large foot. Which one is best for walking across a soft substance, such as sand or snow? Why?

(The answers are on page 24.)

Science Words

Arctic (ARK-tic) the northernmost area on Earth, which includes the Arctic Ocean and the North Pole

hoof (HUF) a hard covering on the foot of an animal, such as a reindeer or horse

lichen (LYE-kuhn) small, tough, plantlike living things that grow on rocks and on trees

mating season (MAYT-ing SEE-zuhn) the time of year when animals come together to have young

migrate (MYE-grayt) to move from one place to another during the year

tundra (TUHN-druh) cold, rocky, treeless land where few plants grow

Index

Read More

Marsico, Katie. *Reindeer (A Day in the Life: Polar Animals).* Chicago: Heinemann Library (2012).

Miller, Sara Swan. *Caribou of the Arctic (Brrr! Polar Animals).* New York: PowerKids Press (2009).

Roman, Patrick. *Caribou (Animals That Live in the Tundra).* New York: Gareth Stevens (2011).

Learn More Online

To learn more about reindeer, visit **www.bearportpublishing.com/ArcticAnimals**

About the Author

Dee Phillips lives near the ocean on the southwest coast of England. She develops and writes nonfiction and fiction books for children of all ages.

Answers

Page 18: A reindeer calf is not as strong as an adult and cannot survive in very cold weather. In spring, the Arctic weather is a little warmer. Also, lots of plants that are easy for the baby to eat and give it lots of energy grow in spring.

Page 22: Your index fingers sank into the sand. That's because all your weight and pressure were pushing on just tiny areas of the sand. When you pushed on the sand with your hands, however, they didn't sink in as much. That's because your weight and pressure were spread over a larger area. Reindeer have large, wide hooves that spread out their weight to stop them from sinking into soft snow.